INTERMEDIATE PIANO DUET • 1 PIANO, 4 HANDS

THE GREATEST SHOWMAN - MUSIC FROM THE MOTION PICTURE SOUNDTF

Arranged for Piano Duet by David Pearl

THE GREATEST SHOWMAN

ISBN 978-1-5400-5524-8

For all works contained herein:
Unauthorized copying, arranging, adapting, recording, Internet posting, public performance,
or other distribution of the music in this publication is an infringement of copyright.
Infringers are liable under the law.

Visit Hal Leonard Online at
www.halleonard.com

Contact us:
Hal Leonard
7777 West Bluemound Road
Milwaukee, WI 53213
Email: info@halleonard.com

In Europe, contact:
Hal Leonard Europe Limited
42 Wigmore Street
Marylebone, London, W1U 2RN
Email: info@halleonardeurope.com

In Australia, contact:
Hal Leonard Australia Pty. Ltd.
4 Lentara Court
Cheltenham, Victoria, 3192 Australia
Email: info@halleonard.com.au

3 THE GREATEST SHOW

10 A MILLION DREAMS

18 COME ALIVE

24 THE OTHER SIDE

27 NEVER ENOUGH

30 THIS IS ME

38 REWRITE THE STARS

43 TIGHTROPE

54 FROM NOW ON

THE GREATEST SHOW

Ladies and gents,
this is the moment you've waited for...

Words and Music by BENJ PASEK,
JUSTIN PAUL and RYAN LEWIS

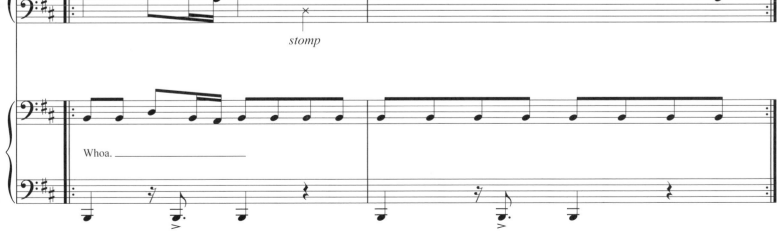

Copyright © 2017 Breathelike Music, Pick In A Pinch Music, T C F Music Publishing, Inc., Warner-Tamerlane Publishing Corp. and Spokane Boy Music
This arrangement Copyright © 2019 Breathelike Music, Pick In A Pinch Music, T C F Music Publishing, Inc., Warner-Tamerlane Publishing Corp. and Spokane Boy Music
All Rights for Breathelike Music and Pick In A Pinch Music Administered Worldwide by Kobalt Songs Music Publishing
All Rights for Spokane Boy Music Administered by Warner-Tamerlane Publishing Corp.
All Rights Reserved   Used by Permission

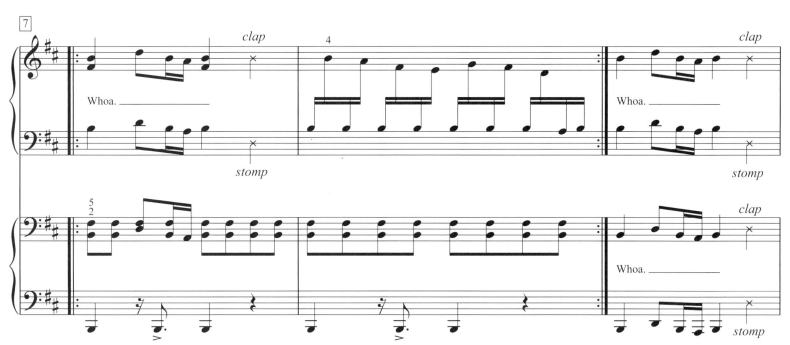

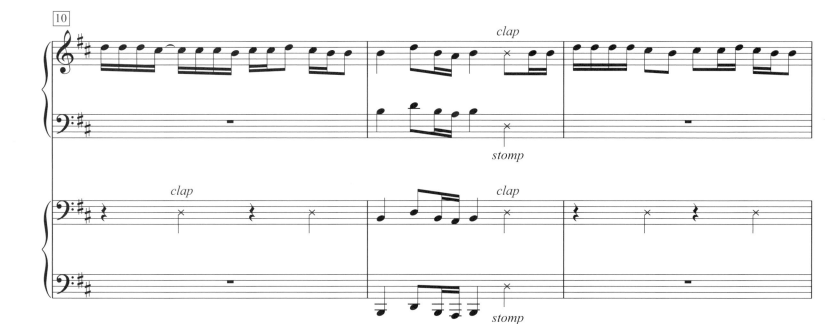

8

CODA

45

48

stomp

stomp

* Optional tremolo with fingers and feet.

A MILLION DREAMS

I close my eyes and I can see
A world that's waiting up for me...

Words and Music by BENJ PASEK
and JUSTIN PAUL

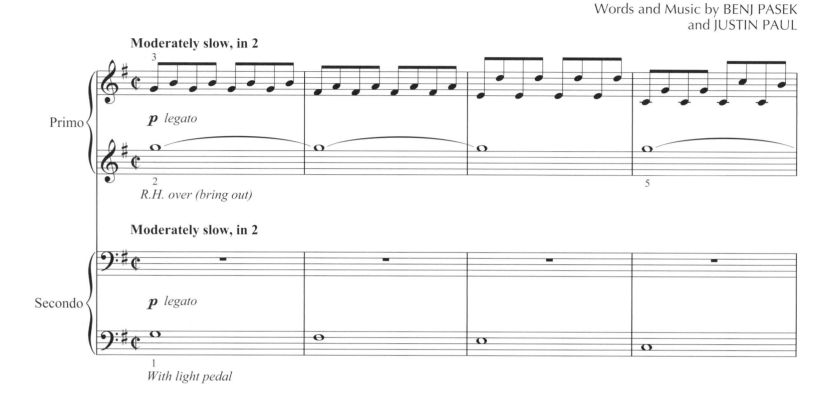

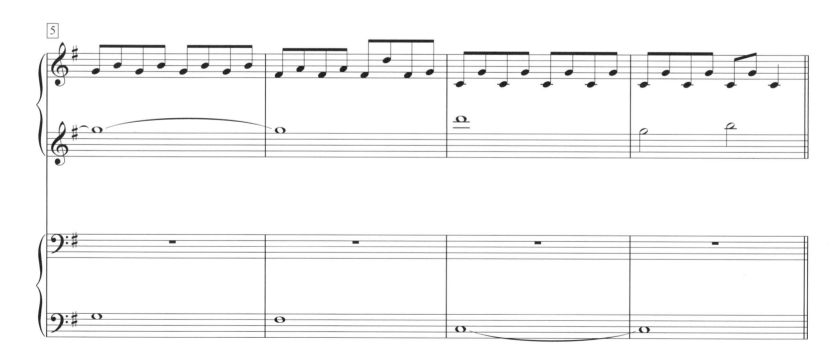

Copyright © 2017 Breathelike Music, Pick In A Pinch Music and T C F Music Publishing, Inc.
This arrangement Copyright © 2019 Breathelike Music, Pick In A Pinch Music and T C F Music Publishing, Inc.
All Rights for Breathelike Music and Pick In A Pinch Music Administered Worldwide by Kobalt Songs Music Publishing
All Rights Reserved   Used by Permission

...Oh, a mil - lion dreams_ for the world we're gon - na make.__ How - ev - er

cresc. poco a poco

D.S. al Coda

D.S. al Coda

CODA

A mil - lion dreams ___ for the world we're gon - na make. ___

...for the world we're gon - na make. ___

COME ALIVE

Come one, come all, come in, come on
To anyone who's bursting with a dream...

Words and Music by BENJ PASEK
and JUSTIN PAUL

Copyright © 2017 Breathelike Music, Pick In A Pinch Music and T C F Music Publishing, Inc.
This arrangement Copyright © 2019 Breathelike Music, Pick In A Pinch Music and T C F Music Publishing, Inc.
All Rights for Breathelike Music and Pick In A Pinch Music Administered Worldwide by Kobalt Songs Music Publishing
All Rights Reserved   Used by Permission

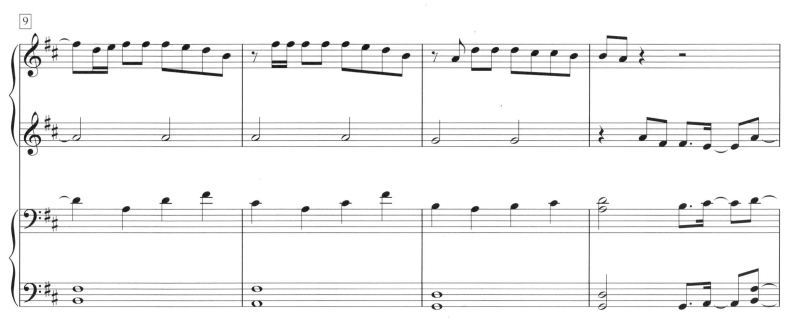

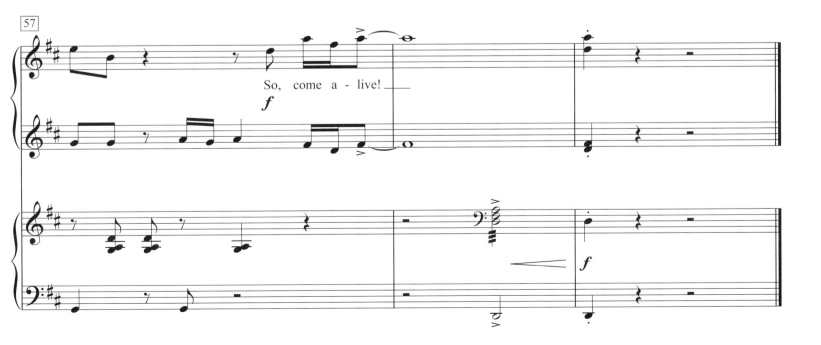

So, come a - live!

THE OTHER SIDE

You can play it sensible, a king of conventional
Or you can risk it all and see.

Words and Music by BENJ PASEK
and JUSTIN PAUL

Copyright © 2017 Breathelike Music, Pick In A Pinch Music and T C F Music Publishing, Inc.
This arrangement Copyright © 2019 Breathelike Music, Pick In A Pinch Music and T C F Music Publishing, Inc.
All Rights for Breathelike Music and Pick In A Pinch Music Administered Worldwide by Kobalt Songs Music Publishing
All Rights Reserved   Used by Permission

We're go - in' to the oth - er side.

...go - in' to the oth - er side.

NEVER ENOUGH

All the shine of a thousand spotlights,
All the stars we steal from the night sky will never be enough.

Words and Music by BENJ PASEK
and JUSTIN PAUL

Copyright © 2017 Breathelike Music, Pick In A Pinch Music and T C F Music Publishing, Inc.
This arrangement Copyright © 2019 Breathelike Music, Pick In A Pinch Music and T C F Music Publishing, Inc.
All Rights for Breathelike Music and Pick In A Pinch Music Administered Worldwide by Kobalt Songs Music Publishing
All Rights Reserved   Used by Permission

THIS IS ME

I won't let them break me down to dust
I know that there's a place for us
For we are glorious.

Words and Music by BENJ PASEK
and JUSTIN PAUL

Copyright © 2017 Breathelike Music, Pick In A Pinch Music and T C F Music Publishing, Inc.
This arrangement Copyright © 2019 Breathelike Music, Pick In A Pinch Music and T C F Music Publishing, Inc.
All Rights for Breathelike Music and Pick In A Pinch Music Administered Worldwide by Kobalt Songs Music Publishing
All Rights Reserved   Used by Permission

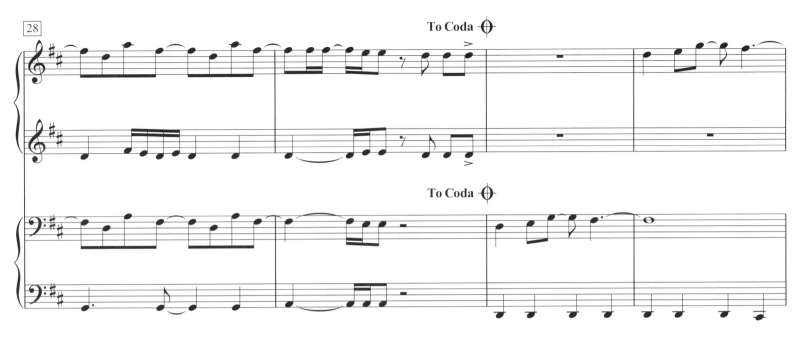

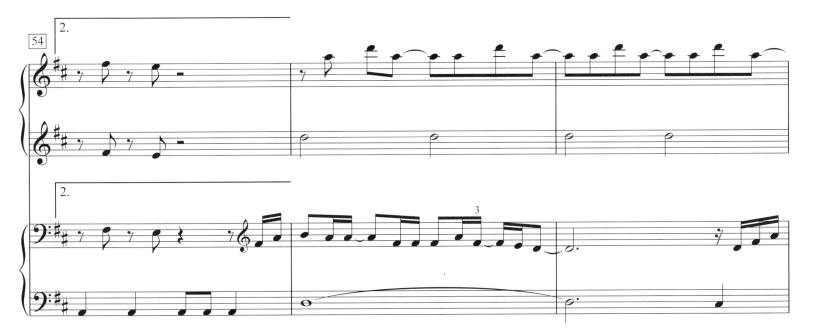

REWRITE THE STARS

It's up to you and it's up to me
No one can say what we get to be.

Words and Music by BENJ PASEK
and JUSTIN PAUL

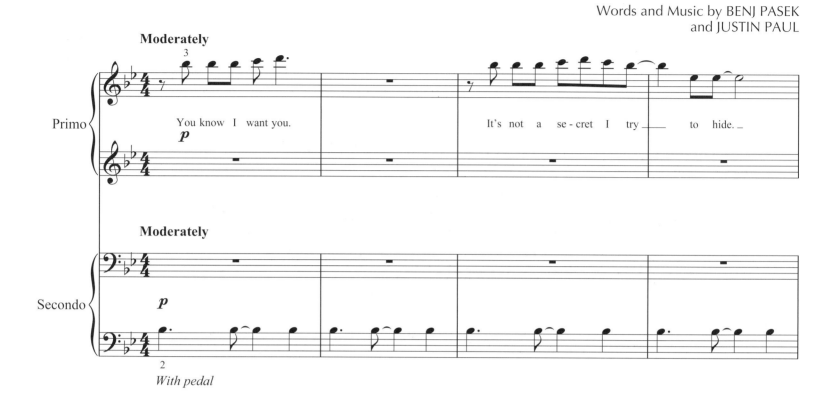

Copyright © 2017 Breathelike Music, Pick In A Pinch Music and T C F Music Publishing, Inc.
This arrangement Copyright © 2019 Breathelike Music, Pick In A Pinch Music and T C F Music Publishing, Inc.
All Rights for Breathelike Music and Pick In A Pinch Music Administered Worldwide by Kobalt Songs Music Publishing
All Rights Reserved   Used by Permission

39

What if we

re - write __ the stars? __ Say you were made to __ be mine? __ Noth - ing could

keep us __ a - part, __ you'd be the one __ I was meant __ to find. __

CODA

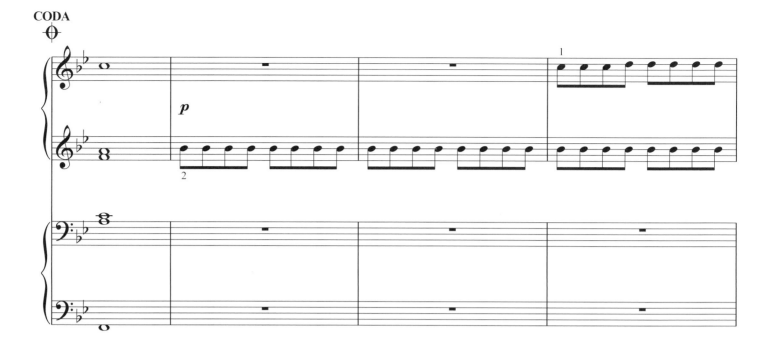

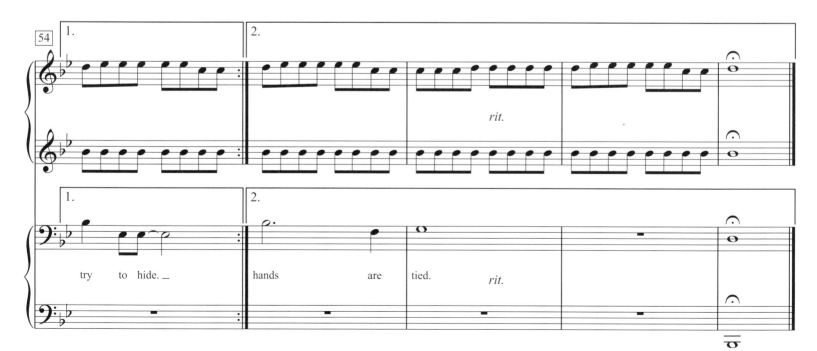

TIGHTROPE

Some people long for a life that is simple and planned
Some people won't sail the sea 'cause they're safer on land
But I'd follow you to the great unknown...
Off to a world we call our own.

Words and Music by BENJ PASEK
and JUSTIN PAUL

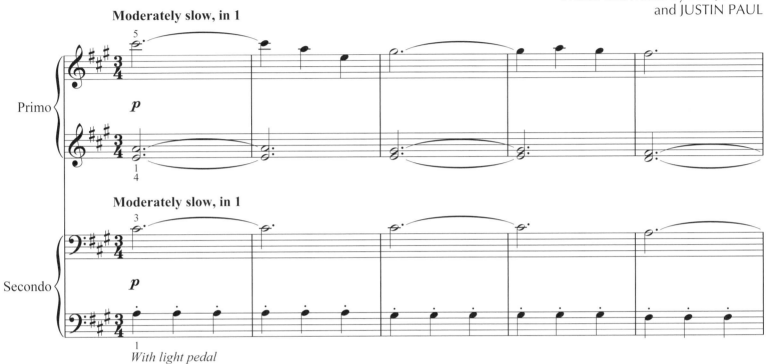

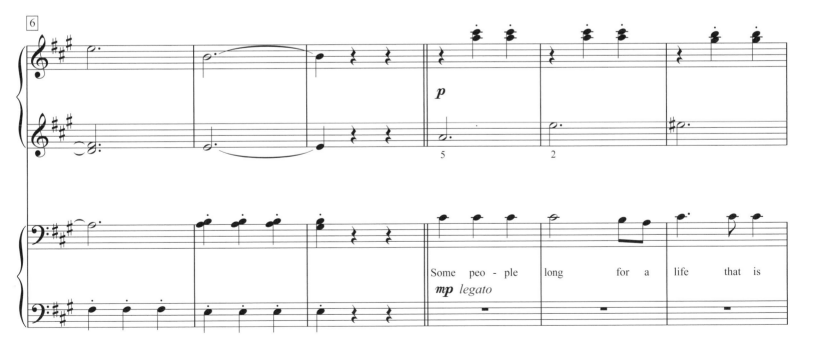

Copyright © 2017 Breathelike Music, Pick In A Pinch Music and T C F Music Publishing, Inc.
This arrangement Copyright © 2019 Breathelike Music, Pick In A Pinch Music and T C F Music Publishing, Inc.
All Rights for Breathelike Music and Pick In A Pinch Music Administered Worldwide by Kobalt Songs Music Publishing
All Rights Reserved   Used by Permission

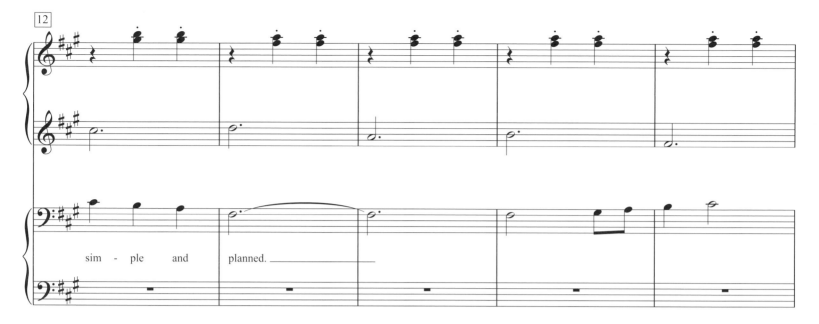

sim - ple and planned._____

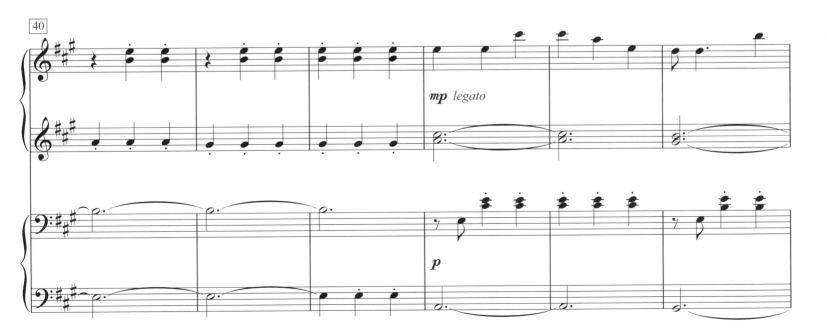

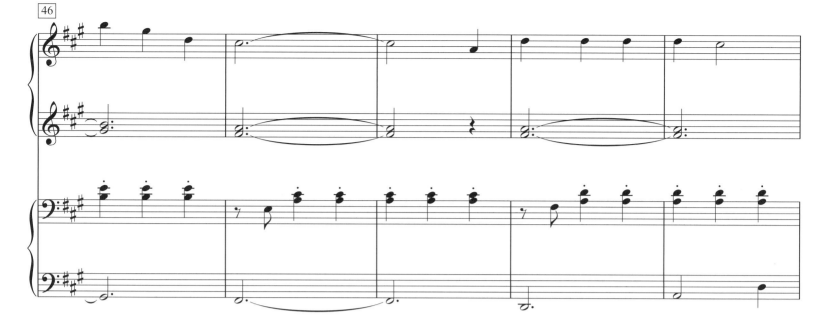

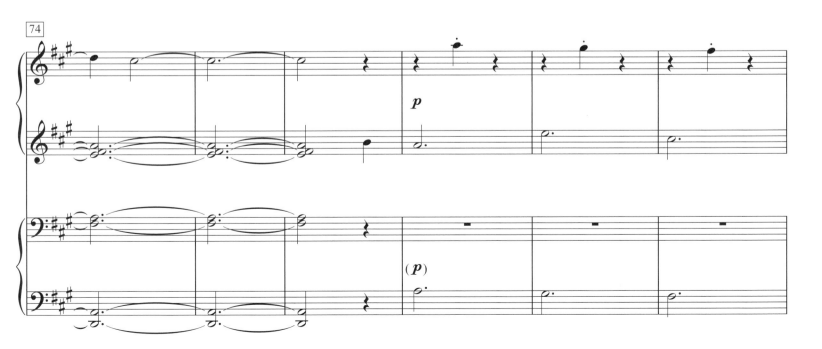

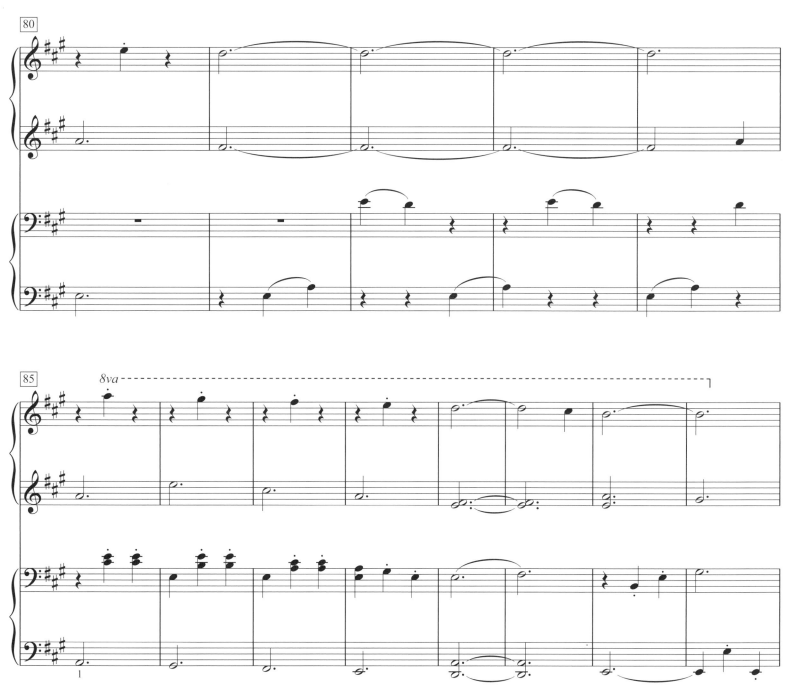

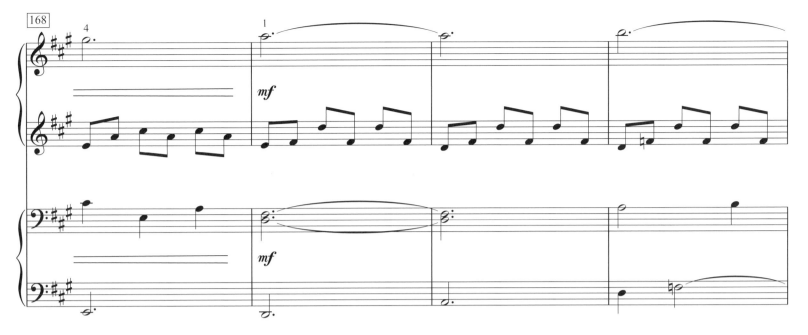

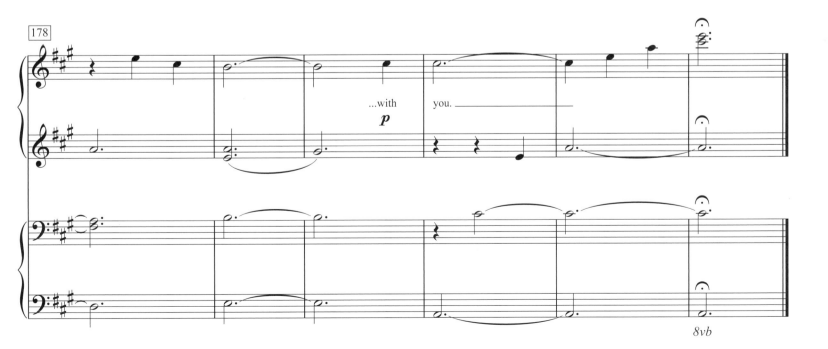

...with you.

8vb

FROM NOW ON

When I stop and see you here
I remember who all this was for.

Words and Music by BENJ PASEK
and JUSTIN PAUL

Copyright © 2017 Breathelike Music, Pick In A Pinch Music and T C F Music Publishing, Inc.
This arrangement Copyright © 2019 Breathelike Music, Pick In A Pinch Music and T C F Music Publishing, Inc.
All Rights for Breathelike Music and Pick In A Pinch Music Administered Worldwide by Kobalt Songs Music Publishing
All Rights Reserved   Used by Permission

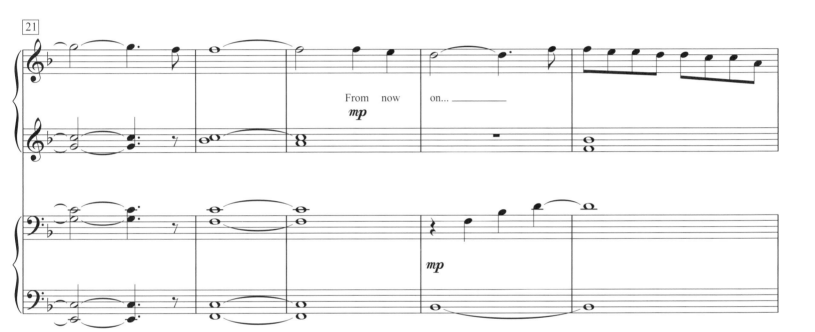

From now on... _____

mp

mp

From now on...

PIANO FOR TWO
A Variety of Piano Duets from Hal Leonard

ADELE FOR PIANO DUET
Intermediate Level

Eight of Adele's biggest hits arranged especially for intermediate piano duet! Featuring: Chasing Pavements • Hello • Make You Feel My Love • Rolling in the Deep • Set Fire to the Rain • Skyfall • Someone Like You • When We Were Young.
00172162 1 Piano, 4 Hands................................$14.99

THE BEATLES FOR PIANO DUET
Intermediate Level
arr. Eric Baumgartner

Eight great Beatles' songs arranged for piano duet! Titles: Blackbird • Come Together • In My Life • Lucy in the Sky with Diamonds • Michelle • Ob-la-di, Ob-la-da • While My Guitar Gently Weeps • Yellow Submarine.
00275877 1 Piano, 4 Hands $14.99

THE BIG BOOK OF PIANO DUETS

24 great piano duet arrangements! Includes: Beauty and the Beast • Clocks • Edelweiss • Georgia on My Mind • He's a Pirate • Let It Go • Linus and Lucy • Moon River • Yellow Submarine • You are the Sunshine of My Life • and more!
00232851 1 Piano, 4 Hands................................ $17.99

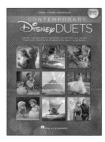

CONTEMPORARY DISNEY DUETS
Intermediate Level

8 great Disney duets: Evermore (from Beauty and the Beast) • How Does a Moment Last Forever (from Beauty and the Beast) • How Far I'll Go (from Moana) • Lava • Let It Go (from Frozen) • Proud Corazon (from Coco) • Remember Me (from Coco) • You're Welcome (from Moana).
00285562 1 Piano, 4 Hands..............................$12.99

EASY CLASSICAL DUETS
Book/Online Audio
Willis Music

7 great piano duets to perform at a recital, play-for-fun, or sightread: By the Beautiful Blue Danube (Strauss) • Eine kleine Nachtmusik (Mozart) • Hungarian Rhapsody No. 5 (Liszt) • Morning from Peer Gynt (Grieg) • Rondeau (Mouret) • Sleeping Beauty Waltz (Tchaikovsky) • Surprise Symphony (Haydn). Includes online audio tracks for the primo and secondo part for download or streaming.
00145767 1 Piano, 4 Hands..............................$12.99

FAVORITE DISNEY SONGS FOR PIANO DUET
Early Intermediate Level

8 great Disney songs creatively arranged for piano duet: Can You Feel the Love Tonight • Do You Want to Build a Snowman • A Dream Is a Wish Your Heart Makes • Supercalifragilisticexpialidocious • That's How You Know • When Will My Life Begin? • You'll Be in My Heart • You've Got a Friend in Me.
00285563 1 Piano, 4 Hands..............................$14.99

FIRST 50 PIANO DUETS YOU SHOULD PLAY

Includes: Autumn Leaves • Bridge over Troubled Water • Chopsticks • Fields of Gold • Hallelujah • Imagine • Lean on Me • Theme from "New York, New York" • Over the Rainbow • Peaceful Easy Feeling • Singin' in the Rain • A Thousand Years • What the World Needs Now Is Love • You Raise Me Up • and more.
00276571 1 Piano, 4 Hands $19.99

GOSPEL DUETS
The Phillip Keveren Series

Eight inspiring hymns arranged by Phillip Keveren for one piano, four hands, including: Church in the Wildwood • His Eye Is on the Sparrow • In the Garden • Just a Closer Walk with Thee • The Old Rugged Cross • Shall We Gather at the River? • There Is Power in the Blood • When the Roll Is Called up Yonder.
00295099 1 Piano, 4 Hands $12.99

THE GREATEST SHOWMAN
by Benj Pasek & Justin Paul
Intermediate Level

Creative piano duet arrangements for the songs: Come Alive • From Now On • The Greatest Show • A Million Dreams • Never Enough • The Other Side • Rewrite the Stars • This Is Me • Tightrope.
00295078 1 Piano, 4 Hands............................ $16.99

BILLY JOEL FOR PIANO DUET
Intermediate Level

8 of the Piano Man's greatest hits – perfect as recital encores, or just for fun! Titles: It's Still Rock and Roll to Me • Just the Way You Are • The Longest Time • My Life • New York State of Mind • Piano Man • She's Always a Woman • Uptown Girl.
00141139 1 Piano, 4 Hands $14.99

HEART AND SOUL & OTHER DUET FAVORITES

8 fun duets arranged for two people playing on one piano. Includes: Any Dream Will Do • Chopsticks • Heart and Soul • Music! Music! Music! (Put Another Nickel In) • On Top of Spaghetti • Raiders March • The Rainbow Connection • Y.M.C.A..
00290541 1 Piano, 4 Hands $12.99

RHAPSODY IN BLUE
George Gershwin/ arr. Brent Edstrom

Originally written for piano and jazz band, "Rhapsody in Blue" was later orchestrated by Ferde Grofe. This intimate adaptation for piano duet delivers access to advancing pianists and provides an exciting musical collaboration and adventure!
00125150 1 Piano, 4 Hands $14.99

RIVER FLOWS IN YOU & OTHER SONGS FOR PIANO DUET
Intermediate Level

10 great songs including the title song and: All of Me (Piano Guys) • Bella's Lullaby • Beyond • Chariots of Fire • Dawn • Forrest Gump - Main Title (Feather Theme) • Primavera • Somewhere in Time • Watermark.
00141055 1 Piano, 4 Hands $12.99

TOP HITS FOR EASY PIANO DUET
Book/Online Audio
arr. David Pearl

10 great songs with backing tracks: Despacito (Justin Bieber ft. Luis Fonsi & Daddy Yankee) • Havana (Camila Cabello ft. Young Thug • High Hopes (Panic! At the Disco) • A Million Dreams (The Greatest Showman) • Perfect (Ed Sheeran) • Senorita (Camila Cabello & Shawn Mendes) • Shallow (Lady Gaga & Bradley Cooper) • Someone You Loved (Lewis Capaldi) • Speechless (Aladdin) • Sucker (Jonas Brothers).
00326133 1 Piano, 4 Hands..............................$12.99

HAL•LEONARD®
www.halleonard.com

0322
054

YOUR FAVORITE MUSIC
ARRANGED FOR PIANO SOLO

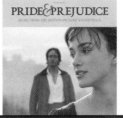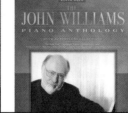

ARTIST, COMPOSER, TV & MOVIE SONGBOOKS

Adele for Piano Solo
00307585...............................$17.99

The Beatles Piano Solo
00294023...............................$17.99

A Charlie Brown Christmas
00313176...............................$17.99

Paul Cardall – The Hymns Collection
00295925...............................$24.99

Coldplay for Piano Solo
00307637...............................$17.99

Selections from Final Fantasy
00148699...............................$19.99

Alexis Ffrench – The Sheet Music Collection
00345258...............................$19.99

Game of Thrones
00199166...............................$19.99

Hamilton
00354612...............................$19.99

Hillsong Worship Favorites
00303164...............................$14.99

How to Train Your Dragon
00138210...............................$22.99

Elton John Collection
00306040...............................$24.99

La La Land
00283691...............................$14.99

John Legend Collection
00233195...............................$17.99

Les Misérables
00290271...............................$19.99

Little Women
00338470...............................$19.99

Outlander: The Series
00254460...............................$19.99

The Peanuts® Illustrated Songbook
00313178...............................$29.99

Astor Piazzolla – Piano Collection
00285510...............................$19.99

Pirates of the Caribbean – Curse of the Black Pearl
00313256...............................$19.99

Pride & Prejudice
00123854...............................$17.99

Queen
00289784...............................$19.99

John Williams Anthology
00194555...............................$24.99

George Winston Piano Solos
00306822...............................$22.99

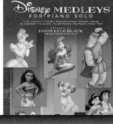

MIXED COLLECTIONS

Beautiful Piano Instrumentals
00149926...............................$16.99

Best Jazz Piano Solos Ever
00312079...............................$24.99

Best Piano Solos Ever
00242928...............................$19.99

Big Book of Classical Music
00310508...............................$24.99

Big Book of Ragtime Piano
00311749...............................$22.99

Christmas Medleys
00350572...............................$16.99

Disney Medleys
00242588...............................$17.99

Disney Piano Solos
00313128...............................$17.99

Favorite Pop Piano Solos
00312523...............................$16.99

Great Piano Solos
00311273...............................$16.99

The Greatest Video Game Music
00201767...............................$19.99

Most Relaxing Songs
00233879...............................$17.99

Movie Themes Budget Book
00289137...............................$14.99

100 of the Most Beautiful Piano Solos Ever
00102787...............................$29.99

100 Movie Songs
00102804...............................$29.99

Peaceful Piano Solos
00286009...............................$17.99

Piano Solos for All Occasions
00310964...............................$24.99

River Flows in You & Other Eloquent Songs
00123854...............................$17.99

Sunday Solos for Piano
00311272...............................$17.99

Top Hits for Piano Solo
00294635...............................$14.99

HAL•LEONARD®

View songlists online and order from your favorite music retailer at
halleonard.com

Prices, content, and availability subject to change without notice.

Disney characters and artwork TM & © 2021 Disney

0422
195